Tudor Colouring Book

Kate Murray

Copyright © 2017 Kate Murray

All rights reserved.

ISBN: 1974254984
ISBN-13: 978-1974254989

DEDICATION

Judith you know this would never have happened without you.

Thank you xx

CONTENTS

Acknowledgments	i
Why Colour?	1
Henry VIII's Rhyme	3
Henry VII	5
Henry VII's Coat of Arms	7
Tudor Peasants	9
Henry VIII	11
Henry VIII's Coat of Arms	13
The Banquet	15
Catherine of Aragon	17
Anne Boleyn	19
Jane Seymour	21
Anne of Cleves	23
Catherine Howard	25
Catherine Parr	27
Hunting	29
Mary I	31
Mary I and Philip of Spain's Coat of Arms	33
Elizabeth I	35
Edward VI	37

ACKNOWLEDGMENTS

A huge thank you to my mum, who also does all my editing, she supports me through all my mad ideas.

A massive thank you to Roland for putting up with my absent stares and odd questions.

1
WHY COLOUR?

Colouring is for kids – right?

Not necessarily.

Adults are getting into colouring in a big way. It's said to relieve stress and anxiety, even lower your blood pressure. It's definitely cathartic. So – you can colour geometric shapes with your morning coffee – if you want to, but free spirits are looking for something more, so what about a Tudor colouring book?

The pen outlines in this book are taken from old paintings and motifs to provide an individual and historically accurate experience.

Why not sharpen up your pencils and your creativity to produce your own art pictures, pictures that celebrate the greatest art form of all, the human body?

Every page is designed so it can be cut out and framed or given away to a friend. Simply colour them in to produce a unique gift.

This is a rhyme from my childhood. It was taught to us to remember what had happened to Henry VIII's wives. Although I always got them muddled…

King Henry VIII,

To six wives he was wedded.

One died, one survived,

Two divorced, two beheaded.

Henry VII

Born 28th January 1457

Died 21st April 1509

He came to the throne on 22nd August 1485 and was the first Tudor monarch.

How did he become King?

By defeating Richard III at the Battle of Bosworth Field which signaled the end of the War of the Roses. He married Elizabeth of York in order to cement his claim to the throne. Thereby creating the Tudor Rose, a mix of the red rose and the white.

Henry's Children

The King had seven children:

- Arthur (Prince of Wales)
19 September 1486 – 2 April 1502
(First husband to Catherine of Aragon)
- Margaret Tudor (Queen of Scots)
28 November 1489 – 18 October 1541
- Henry VIII (King of England)
28 June 1491 – 28 January 1547
- Elizabeth
2 July 1492 – 14 September 1495
- Mary (Queen of France by marrying Louix XII, and the grandmother of Lady Jane Grey)
18 March 1496 – 25 June 1533
- Edmund
21 February 1499 – 10 February 1503
- Katherine
2 February 1503 – 10 February 1503

Henry's wife, Elizabeth, died in childbirth.

Tudor Colouring Book

Kate Murray

This is Henry VII's Coat of Arms.

Tudor Colouring Book

Tudor peasant costume was a simple affair of dresses and jerkins. Here a family poses outside a traditional Tudor building. Luckily for me they didn't mind being drawn...

Henry VIII

Born 28th June 1491
Died 28th January 1547
Henry VIII came to the throne on 21st April 1509 after his father's death.

Henry is known for his six marriages. The first resulted in a disagreement between the Pope and the King, resulting in the English Reformation that separated the Church of England from papal authority and allowed Henry to become Supreme Head of the Church of England. As a result Henry was able to annul his marriage to Catherine of Aragon, but was excommunicated, although still a believer in the Catholic theology. Despite the view today that Henry VIII was large and with a number of medical problems, he was actually an active man. It wasn't until old age that he became obese and had health issues.

Wives and Children

Catherine of Aaragon (married 11 June 1509 – annulled 23 May 1533) Annulled
- Henry Duke of Cornwall (1 January 1511 – 22 February 1511)
- Queen Mary I (18February 1516 – 17 November 1558) Married Philip II of Spain

Anne Boleyn (married 25 January 1533 – annulled 17 May 1536) Beheaded on 19 May 1536
- Queen Elizabeth I (7 September 1533 – 24 March 1603)

Jane Seymour (married 30 May 1536 and died 24 October 1537)
- King Edward VI (12 October 1537 – 6 July 1553)

Anne of Cleves (married 6 January 1540 – annulled 9 July 1540)

Catherine Howard (married 28 July 1540 – annulled 23 November 1541)
Beheaded on 13 February 1542

Catherine Parr (married 12 July 1543)
Henry VIII died 28 January 1547

Tudor Colouring Book

Henry VIII's coat of arms during his later reign.

Tudor Colouring Book

A banquet at Henry VIII's court in all its opulence and grandeur. The party is one of the meeting between Henry VIII and Anne Boleyn.

Based on the painting 'The Banquet of Henry VIII in York Place' (Whitehall Palace) (painted in 1832) by James Stephanoff (1788-1874). Stephanoff became the official 'Historical Painter in Watercolors' to King William IV.

Kate Murray

Catherine of Aragon

Born 16th December 1485
Died 7th January 1536
Queen of England from June 1509 until May 1533

She was married to Henry's elder brother, Arthur, and had the title Princess of Wales. After his death she married Henry VIII.

Catherine is the daughter of Isabella I of Castile and Ferdinand II of Aragon. She was three when she was betrothed to Arthur.

In 1501 she married Arthur but on the 2nd April 1502 he died.

In 1507 Catherine became the ambassador of the Aragonese Crown in England, and the first female ambassador in European history.

In 1509 she married Henry VIII.

In 1513 Catherine was regent of England while Henry was in France for 6 months. During that time England won the Battle of Flodden, where she played an important part.

By 1525 Henry had met and become obsessed with Anne Boleyn. Dissatisfied with his marriage and not having a male heir, Henry set about events to annul the marriage and ultimately break away from the Catholic Church.

In 1533 the marriage was annulled, Catherine never accepted this and always saw herself as the true Queen of England.

On the 7th January 1539 Catherine died and the country went into mourning.

Children
Mary Tudor (born 18 February 1516) would become Mary I

Tudor Colouring Book

Anne Boleyn

Born at some point between 1501-1507
Died 19th May 1536

Anne was the second wife to Henry VIII.

She was the daughter of Thomas Boleyn, 1st Earl of Wiltshire and Lady Elizabeth Howard. Anne was educated in France and the Netherlands due to the fact she was maid of honour to Claude of France. In 1522 Anne returned to England in order to get married to her cousin, James Butler, 9th Earl of Ormond. But these plans were stopped by Cardinal Wolsey, instead Anne became maid of honour to Catherine of Aragon. In 1523 Anne became secretly engaged to Henry Percy, but again the betrothal was broken by Cardinal Wolsey, and she was sent home.

In 1526 Henry started to pursue Anne, but she refused to become a mistress as her sister, Mary, had been. Henry became obsessed with getting the marriage to Catherine annulled so he could take Anne as a wife. When Henry found the Pope would not annul the marriage he started to make a break from the church.

On 25th January 1533 Henry and Anne married. The newly appointed Archbishop of Canterbury, Thomas Cranmer, declared Henry's marriage null and void on the 23rd May 1533, just five days later Henry and Anne's marriage became valid. The Pope excommunicated both Henry and Cranmer.

Anne was crowned Queen of England on 1st June 1533.

In April 1536 Henry had Anne investigated for treason and on the 2nd May she was arrested and placed in the Tower of London. On 15th May she was tried for adultery, incest and plotting to kill the king, and found guilty. She was beheaded four days later.

Children
Elizabeth Tudor (born 7th September 1533) who became Elizabeth I.

Tudor Colouring Book

Jane Seymour

Born around 1508.
Died 24th October 1537

Jane was the daughter of Sir Joh Seymour and Margery Wentworth. She was also a descendant of King Edward III's son, Lionel of Antwerp 1st Duke of Clarence, making her and Henry VIII fifth cousins.

Jane wasn't highly educated, she could read and write a little but her skills were in needlework and household management. Her needlework was well known for being beautiful and elaborate. Henry VIII was known to have become an enthusiastic embroiderer after her death.

She was known to be gentle and kind. In court she would break up and smooth over conflicts. Although not considered a beauty she was charming.

Jane was Queen from 1536 to 1537. She was the third wife of Henry VIII.

Jane came to the throne after the beheading of Anne Boleyn.

She was died due to postnatal complications less than two weeks after giving birth to Edward, who would become King of England.

Jane is the only wife who was given a Queen's funeral and she is buried next to Henry VIII at St George's Chapel in Windsor Castle.

Children
Edward Tudor (born 12 October 1537) who would become Edward VI

Tudor Colouring Book

Anne of Cleves

Born 22nd September 1515

Died 16th July 1557

Anne was the Queen of England from 6th January to 9th July 1540. She was the fourth wife of Henry VIII.

Henry never met Anne until she arrived for the wedding and although it took place he was much disappointed in her appearance, blaming the artist sent to paint her for the problems.

The marriage was annulled as it was never consummated and as a result Anne was never crown queen consort.

Because Anne never opposed the annulment Henry gave her a large settlement including Richmond Palace.

She was, however, part of Henry's family, being declared a 'beloved sister'.

After arriving in England Anne never left, despite feeling a little homesick at times.

Anne lived to see of coronation of Mary I, outliving the rest of Henry's wives.

Catherine Howard

Born 1523

Died 13th February 1542

Catherine was Queen of England from 1540 to 1541.

Catherine was only sixteen or seventeen when she married Henry, who was 49 on the 28th July 1540. It was almost immediately after the annulment of his last marriage.

But sixteen months later in November 1541 Catherine was stripped of her title.

People of the court describe her as a flighty girl who loved to dance, but would lose interest due to the fact she would get distracted.

She was accused of treason because she did not disclose a relationship she had with one of Henry's favourite courtiers, Thomas Culpeper. A love letter by the Queen's hand was found in Culpeper's rooms.

Catherine had been molested as a child, about 13, by her music teacher. If she had admitted to this then Henry could have annulled the marriage and she would have lived, exiled and disgraced but alive. She refused to admit to a liaison as she said it was rape and therefore not consensual.

Both Culpeper and the music teacher, Dereham, were executed. Culpeper by beheading and Dereham was hung drawn and quartered.

On the 13th February 1542 Catherine was beheaded at the Tower of London.

Henry never annulled their marriage.

Tudor Colouring Book

Catherine Parr

Born around 1512

Died 5th September 1548

Catherine was Queen of England between 1543 and 1547.

She was Henry's sixth and last wife. She outlived him by one year.

Catherine was also the most married English Queen with Henry being her third husband. She married Thomas Seymour after Henry's death.

Catherine was close with all three of Henry's children, taking an active role in educating Elizabeth and Edward. She was also a driving force behind the Third Succession Act (1542) which restored Henry's daughters to the line of succession for the throne.

From July to September 1544 Catherine became regent while Henry was in France on a military campaign. Henry had intended for Catherine to rule until Edward came of ages, but he didn't put it into his will.

In 1543 Catherine published her first book, 'Psalms or Prayers', but she did so anonymously. In 1545 a warrant for her arrest was drawn up by anti-protestant officials who wanted to turn the king against her. But she quickly reconciled with Henry and no arrest happened.

Catherine published 'Prayers of Meditations' under her own name and after Henry's death she published 'The Lamentations of a Sinner'.

She became Elizabeth's guardian following Henry's death.

Henry died on the 28th January 1547 and six months later Catherine married her final husband, Thomas Seymour, but the marriage was short-lived as she dies in September 1548.

Tudor Colouring Book

Hunting

In the Tudor period hunting was more than a hobby, it was an essential part of life. It was seen as an enjoyable and needed as it was considered a necessary change from a gentleman's usual work.

It was seen as an avoidance of idleness. As a male child it was seen as a thing to boast about if your son was capable as a hunter.

However hunting wasn't taken lightly. It was an organized affair that fitted within the larger household. A noble child had to know that money was owed the huntsman and how many bones were needed for the hounds. There were also specialized protocols for different hunts, for example a boar hunt had a special spear and sword.

The animal most often hunted was the stag, although at the time it would have been referred to as the hart. Fox hunting wasn't acceptable for a nobleman, only Yoeman farmers hunted them. When a hart or buck was killed it was used as meat. The hart could be hunted most of the year except mid-winter. Then noblemen went hawking with trained falcons. Law was even passed to stop the looting of eggs from these trained birds.

Mary I

Born 18th February 1516
Died 17th November 1558

Ruled from July 1553 until her death.

Daughter of Henry VIII and his first wife, Catherine of Aragon.

Her younger brother, Edward VI, had succeeded Henry on 1547 but Edward became ill in 1553. Edward tried to stop Mary becoming queen as he was against her Catholicism, and on his death leading politicians tried to proclaim Lady Jane Grey as queen.

Mary mustered a force in East Anglia and deposed Jane, who was beheaded.

In 1554 Mary married Philip of Spain, becoming queen consort of Habsburg Spain on his accession in 1556. She never visited Spain.

Mary restored Catholicism. During her 5 year reign she had 280 dissenters burned at the stake in the Marian persecutions.

After her death protestants began to refer to Mary as Bloody Mary.

Tudor Colouring Book

The coat of arms for Mary I and Philip of Spain.

Elizabeth I

Born 7ᵗʰ September 1533
Died 24ᵗʰ March 1603

Elizabeth was on the phone from 17ᵗʰ November 1558 to her death. She is referred to as the Virgin Queen, Gloriana or Good Queen Bess. She was the last monarch of the House of Tudor. Elizabeth was the daughter of Anne Boleyn and Henry VIII, and for most of her childhood was considered illegitimate after her father annulled his marriage to Anne and had her executed.

While Mary I was on the throne Elizabeth spent almost a year imprisoned on suspicion of supporting protestants. In 1558 Elizabeth came to the throne and decided to rule via counsel, she surrounded herself with advisers. One of the first things she did was to reinstate the protestant church with herself as 'Supreme Governor'. This would eventually evolve into the Church of England. When she came to the throne it was assumed that Elizabeth would take a husband and have heirs in order to continue the Tudor house, but she didn't. She did have a number of courtships but eventually, as she grew older, she became known for her virginity. She attained an almost cult like status. Elizabeth was tolerant about religion and far more moderate in government that her predecessors had been. Elizabeth had a few conspiracies to take her life after the Pope declared her illegitimate in 1570, suggesting that her subjects did not have to follow her rule. But in each case her secret service were able to stop the attack.

By the mid 1580's England couldn't afford to ignore the conflict with Spain. And the defeat of the Spanish Armada in 1588 was a huge military success. Elizabeth's reign is known as the Elizabethan era and is famous for it's playwrights and creatives, such as William Shakespeare and Christopher Marlow. It was also a time of discovery with Francis Drake.

Elizabeth sat on the throne for 44 years and gave the country stability while around her other countries had internal conflict.

Edward VI

Born 12 October 1537
Died 6th July 1553

Edward was King of England and Ireland from 28th January 1547 until his death. He was crowned on the 20th February at the age of nine.

He was the son of Henry VIII and Jane Seymour. He was the first monarch to be raised as a protestant.

Throughout his reign the country was ruled by a Regency Council as he never became old enough to rule himself.

Edwards reign is one of economic issues and social unrest, resulting in riots in 1549.

There were two expensive wars, one with Scotland and the other France.

Edward also saw the creation of a protestant church. Unlike his father he was able to step away from Catholic doctrine and create his own. He abolished clerical celibacy and Mass. There were also compulsory services in English.

In February 1553 Edward fell ill and soon it was found to be terminal. The Council drew up a document that was meant to stop the country becoming Catholic again. He named his first cousin, Lady Jane Grey as his successor, completely ignoring his half-sisters. But this was disputed on his death and Jane was deposed 9 days after becoming queen. Although Mary I tried to reverse her bothers religious plans, Elizabeth I used them as the basis for her own protestant reforms.

Tudor Colouring Book

ABOUT THE AUTHOR

Kate Murray has recently completed her Masters in Creative Writing and is currently working as an illustrator and writer. She has had short stories published in magazines and e-zines, including 'The Lampeter Review', 'Jotter's United', and 'What The Dickens'. She has had short stories included in the 'Twisted Tales 2013' anthology published by Raging Aardvark, and the 'Busker Anthology' and 'Spooky Tales Anthology' published by What the Dickens.

Kate's artwork has been exhibited at the Museum Of Modern Art in Machynlleth where she was selected after entering the art competition and at Aberglasney Gardens as part of the Mid Wales Art group. Her artwork has been published by companies from Norway to Australia and her latest written works have illustrations in them. She has also had a series of line drawings published by Staffordshire Wildlife Trust in their biodiversity action plan.

Kate currently works in the foothill of the Cambrian Mountains where she has a purpose built workshop that she affectionately calls her 'house' as she spends far more time in there than anywhere else.

OTHER BOOKS BY KATE MURRAY

Short Story Collections:

'The Phantom Horse'
A series of short stories and flash fiction from horror to romance. Everything needed for an adult book of fairy tales and stories.

Titles include:
"The Phantom Horse" - nightmare or premonition
"Love and Mud" - a romance on a Welsh smallholding
"Trapped in Amber" - unique earrings with a twist

'Love Just Is'
What is love? The Ancient Greeks knew. Realising there are so many types of love, they gave a name to each one.

In 'Love Just Is' each meaning is explored by short stories. Some are obvious and comforting, some shocking and some disturbingly unpleasant.
Eros explores romance and passion.
Ludus looks at love as a game.
Storge, where family means everything.
Mania sees love as art and obsession.
Pragma allows you to shop for love.
Agape is always selfless.
Philia is an act of friendship.

'Shadows Close'

In October 1983, something happened in Shadows Close. The dead-end road was subject to a week of horror that left the inhabitants shaking with terror. This book documents that week and what happened to each resident.

Unlike other short story collections, the characters appear throughout the book as each household lives through its own terror. Shadows Close has ghosts, killers and heroes; be warned that it is advisable not to read it after sunset.

A young boy decides to protect his mother at all cost; a house slips into the floodplain; a couple find themselves reliving a story that is a hundred years old; a ghost, who killed its own mother, is threatened; a man tries to save his family from the evil which is steadily crawling toward his house.

Written in the lean style of dirty realism the short stories are awash with fear and horror. Set within the confines of one street the stories have a strong narrative framework that allow the location to become as much a character as any of the people in the stories. The threshold has been crossed and Shadows Close is the boundary where the human character is placed under a darkly tinted glass.

Novels

'Truth and Lies'

Mary marries a man picked by her mother in a marriage of convenience, yet sixteen years later she realises that she has to run. Except when she gets home she finds herself fighting to keep her family together and to save her son. She has to decide what lengths she will go to in order to protect him...

'The Gone'

Bitsy walks off a plane to find that Heathrow airport is nearly abandoned. She and two men manage to run, but as they do they find themselves in an apocalyptic Britain where humans have become an endangered species and the world is ruled by The Gone. Can they get to the WHO before it is too late?

The Gone is a gritty apocalyptic horror that began as a serialised blog at https://thegone.wordpress.com/. It slowly evolved into the novel with the help of readers, giving rise to a very different Britain that is a challenge to survive in.

'The Gone 2: Evolution'

Bitsy and Max have left Colin in the hands of Aaron and the scientists but should she go back and rescue him when she knows she must leave those she loves to do it?

Can they work out how to save everyone before it is too late, and they become monsters?

The Gone 2 is a gritty apocalyptic horror sequel to 'The Gone'. It is set in a very different Britain where the monsters are not always visible.

'The Shallow Sea'

Mel is in despair as her life falls to pieces around her. Just in time, an opportunity too good to miss comes her way and she embarks on the 'journey of a lifetime'. Just how crucial this journey will be she has no way of knowing, but it will test her strength, her self-belief and her life... 'The Shallow Sea' is a disaster with a twist and only one woman can work out just how far the conspiracy goes, and hopefully she can do it with her heart intact. 'The Shallow Sea' is a full length novel of 50,000 words.

Colouring Books

'An Adult Colouring Book of Fairytales'

Colouring is for kids - right? Not necessarily. Colouring can relieve stress and anxiety, even lower your blood pressure. It's definitely cathartic. But fairytales are for kids - right? Not necessarily. Fairytales were once stories told around fires for adults, not children. They were scary and frightening, the movies of the past. So have a look at some fairytales for adults. Is the tale of the three pigs not scary?

'An Adult Colouring Book Volume 1'

Colouring is for kids – right? Not necessarily. Adults are getting into colouring in a big way. It's said to relieve stress and anxiety, even lower your blood pressure. It's definitely cathartic. So – you can colour geometric shapes with your morning coffee – if you want to. But free spirits are looking for something more, so what about an 'adult' colouring book? The hand-drawn pen outlines in this book are taken from alternative art photographs to provide an individual experience. Why not sharpen up your pencils and your creativity to produce your own art pictures, pictures that celebrate the greatest art form of all, the human body? The book contains 15 illustrations ready to be coloured. The pages are single sided allowing them to be carefully removed and framed once completed.

Made in the USA
Columbia, SC
02 April 2020